Successful Marketing Plans In A Week

Ros Jay and John Sealey

The Teach Yourself series has been trusted around the world for over 60 years. This series of 'In A Week' business books is designed to help people at all levels and around the world to further their careers. Learn, in a week, what the experts learn in a lifetime.

Ros Jay is a freelance writer and editor who has written several books on marketing and for small businesses, including two *Teach Yourself* titles. She has direct personal experience of writing a marketing plan, having set up and run her own publishing business. She has also worked as a business advisor for small businesses and business startups.

John Sealey is a marketing authority, international speaker, author and marketing coach. He helps businesses attract and keep customers, more profitably, with the least amount of effort. John works to show that an enterprise can thrive using proven marketing ideas to achieve more sales and profits. What he uses in his own business and teaches other business owners isn't just theory, but strategies and tactics that work in the real world.

Successful Marketing Plans

Ros Jay
and
John Sealey

www.inaweek.co.uk

Hodder Education

338 Euston Road, London NW1 3BH.

Hodder Education is an Hachette UK company

First published in UK 1997 by Hodder Education

First published in US 2012 by The McGraw-Hill Companies, Inc.

This edition published 2012.

Previous editions of this book were published by Hodder in 1997 and 2003.

British Library Cataloguing in Publication Data: a catalogue record for this title is
available from the British Library.

Library of Congress Catalog Card Number: on file.

10 9 8 7 6 5 4 3

The publisher has used its best endeavours to ensure that any website
addresses referred to in this book are correct and active at the time of going
to press. However, the publisher and the author have no responsibility for the
websites and can make no guarantee that a site will remain live or that the
content will remain relevant, decent or appropriate.

The publisher has made every effort to mark as such all words which it
believes to be trademarks. The publisher should also like to make it clear that
the presence of a word in the book, whether marked or unmarked, in no way
affects its legal status as a trademark.

Every reasonable effort has been made by the publisher to trace the copyright
holders of material in this book. Any errors or omissions should be notified
in writing to the publisher, who will endeavour to rectify the situation for any
reprints and future editions.

Hachette UK's policy is to use papers that are natural, renewable and
recyclable products and made from wood grown in sustainable forests.
The logging and manufacturing processes are expected to conform to the
environmental regulations of the country of origin.

www.hoddereducation.co.uk

Typeset by Cenveo Publisher Services.

Printed and bound by CPI Group (UK) Ltd, Croydon, CR0 4YY.

Also available
in ebook

Contents

Introduction

Nothing can bring a business greater rewards than getting its marketing right. If you have formed a company, it is vital to market your products or services and to make consumers aware of your business. It doesn't matter how good your products or services are if your marketplace doesn't understand what it is you do, why that is going to be of value to them and why they should buy from you and not the competition. Well-thought-out marketing approaches, attached to a good marketing plan, can be the key to your success. Great marketing will grab people's attention, bringing you more customers, more sales and more profits.

The well-known management consultant Peter Drucker once said, 'Whenever you see a successful business, someone once made a courageous decision.' We would add to that wonderful statement, 'attached to a great marketing plan'.

Marketing is at the heart of every successful company. Your business will be operating in a competitive market where customers are becoming increasingly demanding. To win the lion's share of customers and thrive in an ever-changing environment, you need a tailored strategy that will give you an all-important competitive edge. For this, your key driver has to be your marketing plan.

Businesses may fail for many reasons, but a common one is the lack of a marketing plan. Many businesses operating without a plan are surviving by accident. Some business owners know the value of a good marketing plan but have no idea how to create one, while others think it will have little value. Many failed businesses have been found to have had plans for their marketing, but hidden away and never used to help their business survive.

By contrast, the businesses that create, implement and work continually with their marketing plan find that sales and profits materialize more quickly and easily. With this vital tool a business can position itself so as to have prospective customers seeing it as a natural choice. The marketing plan can then be used to help ensure its long-term growth and prosperity, and eventual market domination.

The way you market your company's brand, products and services can mean the difference between you or your competitor getting the sale. Having a good marketing plan in place and enabled will not only unlock huge potential for your business but also help you run your enterprise more smoothly and effectively.

While some businesses may fail to recognize the value of marketing planning, banks and financial institutions don't make the same mistake. A business that tries to apply for a loan or a grant without a good marketing plan is unlikely to get very far.

This book will give you the information and skills you need to develop a sound marketing plan. In a week you will learn how to draw up the kind of plan that not only will impress the bank but can be used as your guide to delivering market awareness and to attracting, winning and keeping sales opportunities.

Ros Jay and John Sealey

SUNDAY

What is a marketing plan?

Marketing is one of the most important aspects of growing your business and is an investment that will pay for itself over and over again. However, business owners often neglect this vital area, either because they underestimate its potential or lack the time and resources, or simply because they misunderstand what a marketing plan is.

So what exactly is a marketing plan? What goes into it? What does it look like? How long does it take to put one together? We'll spend today answering all these practical questions so that, once we start drawing up the plan, you'll know what you're trying to achieve.

Essentially, a marketing plan is like a route map for your business. Every plan will be unique, but it should always cover three basic areas:

- where you are now
- where you are going
- how you are going to get there.

Where you are now

If you're working out a route on a route map, you have to know your starting point before you can work out the best way to reach your destination. So the first stage of drawing up the marketing plan involves establishing precisely where your business is now.

Whether you're starting a new enterprise or running a mature business, your marketing plan needs to take into account your current position. It needs to include information about:

- your product or service
- your customers and prospects
- your competitors
- your business.

We often miss things that we take for granted, but these things can have a profound effect on what will happen in the future. This exercise will identify any areas you'll need to include in your plan, bringing to the fore certain aspects of your marketing that you may otherwise have discounted. This exercise is also vital for another reason: focusing on where you are now will help you see where your strengths and weaknesses may lie.

'You're only as strong as your most important weakness.'

Brian Tracy, renowned business expert

You also need to establish at the start of your marketing plan precisely where you are because other people may want to know. These people might include your bank, anyone you apply to for a loan, advice or grant, or a new business partner. Having the information set out in black and white will turn out to be useful for all sorts of reasons.

This process of taking stock of your current position before you start to think about your goals and objectives will help prevent mistakes and missed opportunities later on. And mistakes can sometimes be expensive in more ways than one.

All too often, people don't think about ways of keeping their business at the cutting edge of customer acquisition. The process of drawing up a marketing plan helps you focus on exactly this sort of potential mistake, so that you can maintain a lead over your competition and position your business as a customer's natural and first choice.

You'll see on Monday and Tuesday that the way you go about putting together this section of the marketing plan is to ask yourself lots of questions. We'll also be looking at how you find out *what* questions to ask. For example, if you identify a weakness in your online marketing, you could ask yourself the following questions:

- How can I include online marketing in my marketing plan?
- Could I tip the scales in the eyes of prospects so that they opt for my offering instead of that of my competition?
- What would be the result on my profits?

Spotting a weakness

One of the things Company X did when establishing its current position was to analyse its weaknesses. Noticing the ever-growing activity of online marketing and everything that goes along with it, the company realized that it had no idea how marketing online might exponentially grow a business.

The company spotted that its competitors had a presence online and appeared to be doing some smart things. The business owner had not given that responsibility to any member of staff, and continued to use current methods even though they were becoming less and less effective.

This ineffective way of trying to educate and win new business was a drain on resources and eventually impacted on his bottom line. He decided to have someone on the team to look after the company's online presence, raise its online profile and attract the sorts of customers the business needed to work with.

TIP *Thinking about where you are now and identifying your weaknesses can help you in your planning.*

And then you go and find the answers – it's as simple as that. Once again, we'll be going into more detail about where and how to find the answers.

Where you are going

We've already established that you can't work out your route if you don't know your starting point. It's equally difficult if you don't know where you're going, so this section of the marketing plan sets this out. There are three main stages in this part of the process.

1 Identify your critical success factors.
2 Set your objectives.
3 Draw up a sales forecast.

Identify your critical success factors

First, you need to establish the factors that are critical to your success. What have you absolutely got to get right in order to succeed and grow? It may not be the end of the world, in some lines of business, if your prices are not particularly competitive – for example, if you sell top-of-the-range designer clothing. But if you run an office stationery business and you can't match your competitors' prices, you could go out of business as a result. You will need to work out which aspects of your business or service are critical.

Establish your marketing objectives

Next you must state your objectives. You will need to draw heavily on the first part of your plan to do this, which is yet another reason for having put down where you are now in black and white.

For example, the first part of your plan may have drawn your attention to a new type of product you could add to your range. Your objectives may include developing this product. If, as in the previous example, you have highlighted the weakness of not being up to date with the advancement of online marketing approaches, this would be one of your objectives.

SUNDAY

MONDAY

TUESDAY

WEDNESDAY

THURSDAY

FRIDAY

SATURDAY

Objectives can be both large and small. The examples above might be relatively small things. Larger objectives that also need to be stated in your marketing plan might be:

- plans for expanding the business
- opening three new branches over the following year
- franchising out the operation
- employing your own sales force instead of using agents.

You will also need to refer to your critical success factors to establish some of these objectives. If you're running an office stationery business, for example, it may be a crucial objective to be able to match your competitors' prices on all frequently ordered products.

Draw up a sales forecast

Then comes the part of your marketing plan where you need to include your sales forecast. Many people find this bit somewhat unnerving, since they don't really know how to forecast sales. They feel they are plucking numbers from the air.

However, there are techniques, which we will examine on Wednesday, for removing much of the guesswork from this process. Of course, there are still some gaps that you will have to fill in with educated guesses, but you can go a long way towards an accurate forecast once you know how.

How you are going to get there

You have established where you are, and you've identified where you want to get to. This final section of the marketing plan explains how you will get from point A to point B. In other words, it states how you plan to achieve your objectives.

This section is, in essence, your marketing strategy. In other words, it is the bit of the marketing plan that contains precise tasks and specific targets.

At this stage, it sounds to most people like an insurmountable challenge to draw up a marketing strategy. But, by Thursday, you'll have collected all the information you need to do it. Then it's just a matter of sitting down and working through it.

By the time you come to draw up the marketing strategy, you'll know how to achieve your objectives in considerable detail. This is a good thing because a marketing strategy is not something to be woolly about. You need to be very specific about how you will achieve each objective, and to consider:

● precisely what you will do to reach each objective
● how often you will do it
● what it will cost
● the results you expect from this action.

As you can see, this is the action plan part of your document. The other parts are crucial, especially if you want information or if something is going wrong and you want to know why. But this final section of the plan is the part you will need to work from on an everyday basis.

The practicalities

The information that goes into your marketing plan therefore covers: *where you are now*, *where you are going* and *how you are going to get there*. What does your document actually look like? And how long will it take to write?

We'll spend Friday answering these questions more fully. As a rough guide, it will probably take you a solid week or two to put the plan together from scratch. This will be less, of course, if you have done some of the work already, or if there is more than one of you working on it.

By the end of this process, aim to have a neat, clear document, smart but simply laid out, and probably 10–25 pages long. It may be longer if your business is complex – if, for example, you sell into several very different markets.

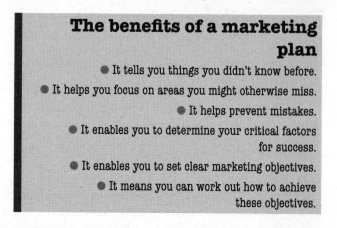

What is the marketing plan for?

The benefits listed in the box above should be enough in themselves to make the process of drawing up the plan worth while. Once you've finished putting it together, you should also use it regularly as one of your most helpful business tools. For example, you can use it in the following ways:

● to show it to people outside the business, such as bank managers, potential investors, advisors, accountants and prospective business partners

● to tell you how your marketing operations are going

● to spot when things have gone wrong, and enable you to put them right.

Summary

Now you know what a marketing plan is and why it's so important to the current and future success of your business. Essentially, it's your route map or guide to growing your business, and it shows you where you are now, where you are going and how you will get there.

The first part is your analysis of where you're starting from: you have to know this before you can work out the best way or ways of reaching your desired destination. The second part tells you where you are going, what your critical success factors and objectives are, and it includes the all-important sales forecast. The final stage of your plan should explain how you're going to get from here...to there, wherever 'there' is for you. It maps out your plan to achieve your objectives.

Your marketing plan should contain exact tasks and specific targets. It'll tell you things you didn't know before, and helps prevent mistakes by determining your critical factors for success and setting clear marketing objectives. It then helps you along the road to achieving those objectives.

Remember
Your marketing plan is part of your overall business plan. Your business plan will take everything else into account.

SUNDAY

MONDAY

TUESDAY

WEDNESDAY

THURSDAY

FRIDAY

SATURDAY

Fact-check [answers at the back]

1. What is a marketing plan?
   a) A document that gives you a view of your overall business ❏
   b) A plan you create once and never look at again ❏
   c) A road map or guide that shares where you are, where you're going and how you'll get there ❏
   d) A measure of your success or failure ❏

2. What is the marketing plan for?
   a) To tell you how successful your business is now ❏
   b) For guiding a business, and for showing investors or the bank ❏
   c) For seeing where you should be spending your money ❏
   d) For describing your administration systems ❏

3. What should your marketing plan include?
   a) A list of suppliers ❏
   b) Nothing about your competitors ❏
   c) Information about your offering, customers and prospects ❏
   d) Information about competitors and your business ❏

4. What are the three main stages to identify where you're going in your business?
   a) Critical success factors, objectives, sales forecast ❏
   b) Talking to a friend, taking advice from a priest, lap of the gods ❏
   c) Suck it and see, pray for the best, survive by accident ❏
   d) Sales, profit, cash ❏

5. What do you need to consider when setting objectives?
   a) What your staff have been up to today ❏
   b) What precisely you will do to reach objectives and how often to do it ❏
   c) What to do about an outstanding invoice ❏
   d) The cost and the results expected ❏

6. What is the best way to determine your marketing weaknesses?
   a) Draw your past history on a whiteboard ❏
   b) Ask your accountant ❏
   c) Identify where you are now and what is missing ❏
   d) Ask yourself lots of questions ❏

7. How often should you refer to your marketing plan?
   a) Once in a lifetime ❏
   b) Once every couple of years ❏
   c) Once every six months ❏
   d) Frequently ❏

8. What is one of the reasons why a business may fail?
a) They don't have a marketing plan ❏
b) They don't care ❏
c) They sold a Rolls Royce when the market wanted a mini ❏
d) Their prices were higher than their competitors' ❏

9. To whom are marketing plans important?
a) Your friends and family ❏
b) Investors and yourself ❏
c) Your neighbours ❏
d) Banks and potential partners ❏

10. How long should a marketing plan take to create?
a) Three months ❏
b) A couple of years if you're lucky ❏
c) About a week with the right tools ❏
d) Between one and three months ❏

SUNDAY

MONDAY

TUESDAY

WEDNESDAY

THURSDAY

FRIDAY

SATURDAY

MONDAY

Asking questions

We've already seen that the first thing you have to do to draw up your marketing plan is to establish where you are now. There are two stages to this: asking the right questions, and finding out the answers. Today we're going to concentrate on the questions.

Obviously, in order to get the most out of today's exercise, you're going to have to know precisely what questions to ask. In order to establish where you are now, you need to ask specific, thoughtful questions about:

- your product or service
- your customers and prospects
- your competitors
- your business.

Questions about your product or service

What exactly is it that you're marketing? You need to describe your product or service range and every variable that it has.

This isn't as pointless as it may sound. We already know that outsiders (such as your investors) may want this information, but you need it too. In fact, you should write it down for the very reason that it seems you shouldn't: there is a strong inclination to take it for granted.

This is the main reason why businesses fail to construct a strong marketing message that fulfils the needs of a market. They take for granted that the marketplace knows what they offer and what their offering will do for them.

YOU ASK THE QUESTIONS

Most companies never question the basic range they offer. But one of the strengths of a marketing plan is that everything in it is open to question whenever you review it. And often – very often – the problem with small companies that are trying to turn into large companies is that their original product range is holding them back. But they don't see it.

The following case study illustrates the type of mistake that companies frequently make. That's why you must ask every possible question, including every possible question about your product and any trends and future trends in your market. That way, you can be sure that, if anything ever needs to change, it will show up at your marketing plan review sessions.

SUNDAY
MONDAY
TUESDAY
WEDNESDAY
THURSDAY
FRIDAY
SATURDAY

Understanding market trends

Steve manages a business that runs training seminars and invites companies to send delegates along. As time goes by, more and more companies ask him to run online seminars – webinars – for them instead; that's the way the trend is going.

After a while, it gets harder to fill the open on-site seminars, which start to lose money. But Steve thinks, 'We're a company that organizes open seminars; we always have been. We must invest more in this side of the business so that it becomes profitable again.' Steve tries harder to sell his seminars, even though the evidence shows that the market has grasped that online seminars are more cost-effective and cheaper for them.

The only way Steve will find out whether he is pouring money into a bottomless pit is from his marketing plan. But the marketing plan will only contain the answers to the questions he asked it.

Ask yourself the following questions, relating to what you offer and how you sell it. These are just some of the possible questions and you may think of more that are relevant to your circumstances.

Questions to ask about your offer

- **What is our product or service?**
  - What is the range?
  - What does it look like?
  - Does it come in a choice of colours or sizes?
  - Are there customized options?
  - Do we sell accessories and add-ons?

- **Where do the raw materials come from?**
  - Are the supplies of good enough quality for our customers?
  - Are they delivered fast enough to fulfil orders on time?

You might think these are manufacturing questions, and you'd be right, of course. But they are also marketing questions.

- **What is the packaging like?**

Once again, this question has a marketing dimension. If your product looks basic, it won't be easy to charge a premium price for it, however good its performance. The packaging may also influence the distribution, making the product too large or too heavy for certain distribution methods.

Questions to ask about selling

- **How is the product transported?**
  - Is transport a problem because of cost, weight, fragility, size or anything else?

- **Where is it sold?**
  - Do we sell direct through mail order?
  - Do we sell from our own premises?
  - Do we sell through a retailer?

- **In what form does it reach the customer?**
  - Is it ready to use, or does it need to be assembled, painted, programmed or whatever?

- **Does it need explaining?**
  - Will the customer understand it, or does it need instructions to go with it? *simple Instructions on packaging*
  - If so, what sort of instructions does it need, and in what format (video, audio, PDF on CD)?

SUNDAY

MONDAY

TUESDAY

WEDNESDAY

THURSDAY

FRIDAY

SATURDAY

● **Is it easy to use?**
- Are there any integral problems that customers might find irritating?
- Does it take a long time to warm up or need recharging three times a week?

● **How easy is it to increase production if sales go up?**
- Will we be caught out having to pay for outsourcing or overtime we can't afford?
- Will we fail to deliver on time?

You can often get round these problems if they occur, but usually at a cost. That's why you need to plan for them.

As you can see, not all these questions apply to every product or service. There may be others that are particularly pertinent to yours. But this is a good general guide, and you should add other questions if you think of them. Another way of coming up with the right questions is to ask a focus group of your 'A class' clients, those who are loyal, love your service or products and are a pleasure to work with. They can ask questions of you that you may never have thought of. In addition, they are asking from their own perspective and for their own benefit.

 TIP *Since you will be reviewing and updating your marketing plan regularly, you can always add information later. But try to cover everything you can from the start.*

Questions about customers and prospects

If you are just setting up a new business or launching a product for a new market, you still have to ask these questions. It's just that in your case all your customers will be potential at the moment. Don't worry; tomorrow we'll find out how to get the answers to these questions even if you don't have a single customer yet.

Who are our customers?
- What age are they?
- ✗ Are they male or female, or both?
- Are they business or private?
- Where do they live?
- What is their income?
- What online forums do they frequent?
- ✗ What are their interests?

What are their buying trends?
- Do they buy more or less than they used to?
- What's the overall market trend?
- Do they buy more or less if they hit hard times?

How much will they pay?
- Would they buy more if it were cheaper?
- Would they pay more if it were better quality?
- How do they like to pay?

How do they know about the product or service?
- ✗ Do they see it in a shop?
- Is it advertised?
- ✗ Is it reviewed in the press?
- ✗ Do we exhibit at trade shows?
- ✗ Do they see it on our website or use search engines to find us?

Where do they buy it?
- ✗ Do they buy in a shop and, if so, what kind of shop?
- Do they buy it through mail order, by phone or via a website?

Questions to ask about customers' attitudes

● **What do they like about our product or service?**
  ✗ What are the features they go for?
  – Is it price, accessories or after-sales service?
  – Does the product have status value?

● **What do they dislike about it?**
What would the people who don't buy from us but from someone else say was wrong with our product or service?

● **What do they like about this type of product or service?**
What are the general benefits that our product shares with the competition? (For example, all people who buy electric egg whisks do so because they are faster and easier than the alternatives.)

● **What do they dislike about this type of product or service?**
Why do our existing customers choose our product or service rather than our competitors'? In other words, what makes us unique? Do they understand our USP or EVP?

USP = Unique Selling Proposition
EVP = Extra Value Proposition

Once again, these questions are not exhaustive, but they should give you a pretty good idea of the kinds of things you need to include in your marketing plan.

It's vital that you also ask the questions you might not like the answers to, such as, 'What do our customers like least about our product or service?' And when it comes to finding the answers, you must be brutally honest. If your competitors are better than you in certain areas, you must acknowledge the fact. These will be some of the areas where you can generate the most improvement, but only if you recognize your shortcomings.

Questions about your competitors

Your satisfied customers are still going to judge you against your competitors constantly and they will be ready to switch allegiance any time it seems worth while. So you had better know what they know. It is much harder to move or woo your loyal customers away from you. Your marketing plan must therefore take into account your satisfied – but open-minded – customers as well as those who remain loyal.

This part of the plan will obviously need revising as competitors change, but for the moment you want to start with a snapshot of what the competition is up to now.

Again, it's extremely important that you also ask yourself all the questions you think you might not want to hear the answers to, such as what your competitors are particularly good at. These are precisely the questions you *need* to know the answers to. Far too many business people fail because they convince themselves that they are wonderful and the competition is hopeless, so there is no need to change.

TIP *The seven most expensive words in business are 'We have always done it this way.' By constantly asking questions, you move away from those seven deadly words.*

Questions to ask about the competition

● **Who are our competitors?**
  - What product or service are our prospects using at the moment?
  - If they aren't buying from us yet, are they buying from someone else?
  - Are they making do without, or using an alternative product?

For example, if you sell electric egg whisks, do your prospects buy from a competitor, use a rotary whisk, use a fork or not eat beaten eggs at all? What proportion of your prospects uses each of these options?

Questions to ask about their offer

● **Do competitors offer anything beyond a basic service or product?**
  - If so, what?
  - Does their product come with extra features?
  - Do they offer a choice of service levels?

● **What have our competitors got that we haven't?**

Another useful exercise to go through when it comes to asking questions about your competitors is to draw up a table like the one below. Allow as many columns as you have main competitors, plus a column for yourself. Allow enough space to fill in each section with the necessary information.

Competitor comparison table

	Your product or service	Competitor 1	Competitor 2
Product or service (what is the range?)			
Price (standard item for comparison)			
Special offers (what are they?)			
Quality (marks out of 10)			
Customer-care skills (marks out of 10)			
Reputation (marks out of 10)			
Delivery (marks out of 10)			
After-sales service (marks out of 10)			
Location (local, regional, national, etc.)			
Advertising (what and where)			

Questions about your business

The final list of questions you need to draw up is about the business itself. These questions are, of course, to do with marketing, but in the broadest terms. They are questions about things that are integral to the whole business. The best way to compile this list is by using SWOT analysis.

If you haven't come across this before, SWOT is simply an acronym for:

- strengths
- weaknesses
- opportunities
- threats.

The process of SWOT analysis involves asking yourself to describe these four factors as they apply to your business. This means describing not how you would like them to be but how they actually are.

The accepted way to do a SWOT analysis of your business is to draw yourself a table like the one below, and then fill in each section with a list of the appropriate points.

SWOT analysis

Strengths	Weaknesses
Opportunities	Threats

We'd better go through the four categories and explain what kind of answers you're going to need to fill in.

Strengths

Your strengths are all to do with internal factors related to the business. You cannot have every strength there is. Being a large company can be a huge strength because it gives you a degree of financial clout that a small business can never have. On the other hand, a small company can have the speed of response and flexibility in customer handling that a multinational can't hope to achieve. You may have a broad customer base or a highly targeted customer list; you are unlikely to have both, and yet both could be strengths. Don't expect everything. Just concentrate on listing the strengths you have now.

You should list *all* your plus points in this quarter of the table: low costs, good technical knowledge or whatever.

Examples of strengths

- Low costs
- Low overheads
- Good location
- Flexibility
- Good internal communications
- Well-motivated staff
- Highly skilled staff
- Good product expertise
- Good market knowledge
- Broad customer base
- Good reputation
- Sound finances
- Up-to-date product/service range
- Up-to-date equipment
- Sophisticated computer system
- Strong online presence

Not all these strengths will be relevant to you, and you may have others. Every business is different. But these examples should have given you a good idea of the kind of things you're looking for. You'll see from this list that, even if yours is a new business, you may already have a number of strengths you can list.

Weaknesses

When it comes to weaknesses, which are also internal factors related to the business, you must be absolutely honest with yourself. You may think you *ought* to have a highly skilled workforce, but if you don't you must list this fact as a weakness. Otherwise it won't get on to the list of things to improve.

You will probably notice that the weaknesses are usually the other side of the 'strengths' coins. If low costs are a strength, for example, high costs would be a weakness.

Examples of weaknesses

- High costs
- High overheads
- Poor location
- Lack of flexibility
- Poor internal communications
- Poorly motivated staff
- Poorly skilled staff
- Overdependence on one or two key staff
- Limited product expertise
- Poor market knowledge
- Small customer base
- Weak reputation

- Poor online presence
- Financially weak
- Out-of-date product/service range
- Out-of-date equipment/machinery
- Computer system that needs upgrading or replacing
- Poor market position

Opportunities

Opportunities are external market forces that impinge on your business in some way. These factors can come from all kinds of sources: customers, competitors, suppliers, EC regulations, government legislation and so on. Only you can know exactly which areas to look at, because each business is different.

Examples of opportunities

- Weak competition (at least in some areas)
- Competitor going out of business or moving away
- Expanding market
- New legislation in pipeline that will be good for the market
- Grants available
- Good new source of raw materials available
- Useful exhibition coming up
- New, skilled staff joining the company
- Using the internet and social media to stay in touch with customers

Threats

As with strengths and weaknesses, threats are often the flip side of opportunities and, like opportunities, they are external forces that may affect your business. As with opportunities, only you can know exactly which areas to look at because each business is so different. Threats can even come from the media; look at the effect the BSE scandal in the 1990s had on the UK beef and dairy industries, largely because of the media interest that surrounded it.

Your particular market may have special threats that don't affect other businesses. But, once again, here are some ideas.

Examples of threats

- Strong competition
- Competitor giving special offers or discounts
- Shrinking market
- New legislation in pipeline that will be bad for the market
- Grants available to competitors
- Important supplier going out of business
- Raw materials going up in price
- Good staff leaving the company
- Expensive legal action pending
- Malware from social media sites that can cripple your IT network

Summary

Today we've looked at the questions you need to ask as soon as you start to put your marketing plan together and at how you can find out about the business itself, using SWOT analysis. The quality and timing of the questions you ask can dramatically change the direction of your business. If your competitors ask the correct questions, find the answers and you don't, they'll have a competitive advantage.

A great question from the late, great Jim Rhon was, 'What am I getting?' He would then ask the same question another way to get a better answer: 'What am I becoming?'

The questions you ask and how you ask them can have immense power. You could go as far as to say asking the right questions at the right time and finding the answers can turn a mediocre business into a legendary one. Use them to solve creative problems, to shift a certain perspective about a challenge your business has, to focus on an issue, to set a goal or to get inspiration.

You may already know the answers to some of the questions we've asked. Tomorrow we'll find out how to go about answering the rest of them.

SUNDAY

MONDAY

TUESDAY

WEDNESDAY

THURSDAY

FRIDAY

SATURDAY

Fact-check [answers at the back]

1. Questions establish what when it comes to your business?
   a) Who will win the next World Cup ❏
   b) Where you are now in your business ❏
   c) What your next company car should be ❏
   d) The issues you need to focus on ❏

2. What questions should you be asking from a marketing plan point of view?
   a) How much can I earn today? ❏
   b) Who will I put on a particular job today? ❏
   c) Questions about my product or service ❏
   d) Questions about selling, customers and prospects, and the competition ❏

3. What is the acronym that will help you identify the strengths, weaknesses, opportunities and threats in your business?
   a) SWOT ❏
   b) FABAC ❏
   c) SPIN ❏
   d) STOW ❏

4. Strengths and weaknesses are to do with what in SWOT?
   a) How strong or weak you personally are ❏
   b) How strong or weak the economy is ❏
   c) How strong or weak your competitors are ❏
   d) Internal factors relating to your business ❏

5. What's a good example of a strength?
   a) That you close your business early on Thursdays ❏
   b) Well-motivated staff ❏
   c) Your response time to customers is lower than average ❏
   d) Good reputation ❏

6. When it comes to weaknesses in your business, what should you be?
   a) Honest with yourself ❏
   b) Taking it with a pinch of salt ❏
   c) Ignoring your weakness ❏
   d) Able to 'muddle through' despite them ❏

7. How will asking questions about your business help you?
   a) It will identify what happened in the past ❏
   b) It will help you put your current marketing plan together ❏
   c) It will enable you to get the answers from your family ❏
   d) It will let you describe how you would like it to be ❏

8. How important is it to ask the right questions?
   a) Not important ❏
   b) Reasonably important if time permits ❏
   c) Not vital, but it helps ❏
   d) Vital ❏

9. What are the seven most expensive words in business?
a) We have always done it this way ❏
b) There are opportunities everywhere if you look ❏
c) Bring me the figures for the last quarter ❏
d) We will look at those questions tomorrow ❏

10. What can questions do?
a) Cause annoyance ❏
b) Help you win game shows ❏
c) Help solve problems ❏
d) Shift your thinking and help you focus ❏

TUESDAY

Researching
the answers

Now you have a very long list of questions with no answers to them – yet. Today is all about researching the answers to the questions we asked yesterday. Some of these are easy to answer, while others will take longer. The important thing is not to guess at any of the answers but to do everything you can to be sure that your answers are accurate.

Today you will learn about the places you can go to for answers to your questions. You can research your answers from:

- existing, off-the-shelf information, which might be from your own records or from external locations such as libraries, trade associations and regulatory bodies, the trade press, government departments or local agencies
- your customers, or potential customers, if you're just starting out in business
- the internet, which may include looking at discussion forums and blogs as well as websites
- other people, such as suppliers, competitors or other businesses.

Off-the-shelf information

The first place to find ready-made information is inside your head. So the first thing to do is to go through the list of questions you drew up and write down all the answers you are sure you already know.

There may be fewer of these than you think. Do you really know that your customers appreciate your fast delivery times? Have they ever said so? Have you ever asked them, or read someone else's research into what matters to customers in your particular market? If not, you are only assuming the information, so don't write anything down just yet. You may well be right about how your customers feel, but we're not writing down guesses and assumptions, we're only writing down known facts.

However, you probably will know the answers to the questions about what your product range is, and about your competitors, and you'll know a lot of the answers to the SWOT analysis.

Once you've written down the answers that you are sure of at this stage, your list of questions should already be starting to look a little more manageable. There are now several other places you can go to find off-the-shelf information that will give you the answers to an enormous number of questions.

Your own records

This is one of the best places to start, and one of the many reasons for keeping thorough customer records.

Assuming you're already in business and have decent customer records, you should be able to extract all sorts of useful information you didn't realize you had. For example, if you look at how your customers responded when you introduced an express delivery service – how many used it regularly, how many used it occasionally, and so on – you can start to answer the questions about delivery times.

Now you know what information you're looking for, you should be able to work out how to extract it from your records. What's more, these records of the way your customers really behave are far more reliable than anything your customers *say* they will do if, for example, you raise your prices, or introduce a fast delivery option.

This is also a good way to establish whether the quality of your customer records is a strength or a weakness. You can now enter that on your SWOT analysis.

Directories and websites

Any main library should have plenty of useful publications. Your local library should be able to direct you to a good business library, and you'll also find much of the information online. These are some of the most useful directories and websites.

- *BRAD (British Rate and Data)*
  - marketing intelligence (www1.bradinsight.com/) with listings of every British newspaper and magazine, from the trade press to local freesheets, with distribution figures, advertising rates and other information about advertising
- **Bureau van Dijk**
  - publisher (www.bvdinfo.com) of company information and good business intelligence. Their databases range from UK company information to comprehensive global coverage
- *The Directory of British Associations*
  - listings (www.cbdresearch.com) of trade associations or societies that could help you
- *Europages*
  - directory (www.europages.com) of in-depth information on 2.3 million companies from 35 countries across Europe. Search by company name, product, business sector, country, company type or number of employees

- **EXPO21XX**
  - directory of online trade exhibitions (www.expo21xx.com) with 'fairs' for industry sectors from textiles to office supplies and everything in between
- **FITA (The Federation of International Trade Associations)**
  - global trade portal (www.fita.org) and a great source of international import and export trade leads and events. This portal links to over 8,000 international trade (export/import) related websites. Focused on the promotion of international trade, import–export, logistics management, finance and a lot more. A wonderful resource to research your competition and your prospective customers

---

Online trade fairs

Contact EXPO21XX to find out when your sector is exhibiting and visit the site then. The 'exhibitions' are subdivided into halls, and each company in the hall has a brief description and a flag of the country in which it is based on their stand. The level of subscription they have with EXPO21XX will determine how much additional information there is on that company. With low-level subscribers, you'll have to use the power of information-gathering questions to get the intelligence you're seeking. In 2012 there were over 1,300,000 'exhibitors'.

- *Kompass*
  - worldwide directory and website (gb.kompass.com/) listing companies by industry, name, product and location
- **Marketsearch**
  - publisher (www.msearch.com) of more than 20,000 market research reports
- *The Municipal Year Book*
  - listings of local authorities including contact names
- *The Retail Directory*
  - listings of large retail and department stores and the names of buyers

- **Solusource**
  - directory (www.solusource.com) of manufacturers and distributors across 28 countries, all classified by around 11,000 products and services categories. Search by product/service or company name or browse categories
- **The Source Book**
  - marketing information by services and industry sectors; it will also tell you about directories and trade associations
- **Wer liefert**
  - business directory (www.wlw.de) with data on companies and their products in Belgium, Germany, Croatia, Luxembourg, Netherlands, Austria, Switzerland, Czech Republic, Slovenia and Slovakia. Search by product, service or company name website, email addresses, postal addresses, contact names or telephone numbers
- **Yellow Pages** and **Thomson Directories**
  - plenty of information about potential customers, competitors and your industry
- **Zibb**
  - portal (www.zibb.com) of over 900 Reed Business titles where you can search for any category by keyword.

Trade associations and regulatory bodies

You can often get useful information from these organizations, which publish annual reports and industry information. Some of them may charge you for this information but, if it's your own industry or a major industry for you to sell into, it could still be well worth it.

Regulatory bodies, such as the Law Society and the British Medical Association, are often good sources of information, along with trade associations. These should all be listed in some of the publications above.

The trade press

BRAD will give you listings of every trade and specialist magazine or newspaper you can imagine. Ring up the ones that are relevant to your business and ask for a copy – the advertising department will often let you have one free along with a rate card. It will be packed with information that is useful to you.

You could even ask one of the editorial staff to answer the odd question if you're really stuck and need someone with industry knowledge. They're usually too busy to answer long lists of questions, but this can be a handy last resort.

Government departments

Go to www.statistics.gov.uk in the UK or FedStats.gov or USA.gov in the US for lists of government publications. You can get a wide range of data including census reports, overseas trade information, data on social trends and so on. If you need information about exporting, contact the Department for Business, Innovation and Skills (BIS) in the UK or export.gov in the US.

Your local enterprise agency

This will be listed in the *Yellow Pages* under 'Business Enterprise Agencies' in the UK or Business Enterprise Programs (BEP) in the US. Each enterprise agency or program is different, but they all give a wealth of advice to new and existing businesses – and it's often free. They can probably tell you about exporting, grants and loans for which you are eligible, relevant legislation and plenty more.

Your customers

If you want to know what your customers and prospects think, the simplest way is to ask them. You can talk to them face to face or on the phone, or you can email or write to them. The three categories of customers you can talk to are:

1 existing customers, to find out why they buy from you
2 potential customers, to find out what would persuade them to buy from you
3 ex-customers, to find out why they stopped buying from you.

Overlying this, you might have more than one group of customers if you sell into more than one market.

I WANT TO KNOW WHY YOU STOPPED BUYING FROM ME!

Talking to your customers face to face

The easiest way to do this is simply to chat to your customers informally when you are doing business with them. You could say, for example, 'We're doing a bit of research at the moment to find out how our customers feel about our delivery service. Could you tell me what you think?'

This is a cost-effective and time-effective way to research your customers, and it often generates useful ideas and suggestions. However, it's hard to build up a large sample of customers or a long list of questions – your customers won't want to answer more than one or two off the cuff. Also, people are less likely to be honest face to face if their views are negative.

Overall, this is a good approach if you're only after the answers to one or two questions, or if you're looking for suggestions.

Telephoning your customers

You can always phone up customers. Tell them what you want and ask them if they can spare the time: 'Hello, Mr Smith. It's Kim Jones here from ABC Ltd. We're trying to find out more about how we can improve our service to customers. I was wondering if you could spare five or ten minutes to answer a few questions?'

This has the advantage that you can ask more questions than you could do face to face, you can ask supplementary questions and you can make sure you ask everyone the same questions. However, it can be both expensive and time consuming if you want to research a large sample of your customers.

Generally, you should use this approach when you need to speak to only a few customers but want to ask several questions and want to be able to quantify the results.

Using written questionnaires

Another option is to ask your customers to fill out a questionnaire. You can hand it out if you meet your customers regularly, or you can send it out with deliveries or bills (in which case you are surveying only these customers who place orders). Alternatively, you can email or post it.

The benefit here is that you can survey a large number of customers relatively cheaply, and you can quantify the results because you have asked them all the same questions. You can also give customers the option of remaining anonymous, which can lead to more honest replies.

General guidelines for research

There are certain fundamental mistakes that novice researchers – understandably – are inclined to make. Research is something that everyone gets better at with practice. Once you find that certain questionnaire answers aren't helpful, you'll learn what type of questions not to ask. Here are a few tips to help you avoid the classic pitfalls.

1 Keep your questions neutral
If you say, 'Are you happy with our delivery service?', most customers will go for the easy option and say yes. Instead, try asking them, 'How would you improve our delivery service?'

2 Don't be ambiguous
If you ask someone 'Do you change your car frequently?' they may think once every five years is frequently, or once

every six months isn't. Ask them the more specific question, 'How often do you change your car?' for a more precise answer.

3 Be consistent if you want to add up the answers
This applies whether you're talking to customers face to face or over the phone. If you ask each customer a slightly different question, you won't be able to add up the answers properly.

4 Don't ask the customer to give up more than five or ten minutes of their time
This applies to both telephone surveys and written questionnaires. If you have a long list of questions you want answered, you can ask one group of customers one set of questions and another group a different set. Choose the groups in a way that will divide them randomly, such as selecting them alphabetically, rather than dividing them according to location or ordering frequency.

5 Use multiple-choice questions on written questionnaires
These are much easier to analyse when you get them back. You can always mix them with other questions if you feel it would be helpful.

6 Don't expect an overwhelming response to postal questionnaires
If you're mailing existing customers, a response rate of between 5 and 20 per cent is very respectable.

CAN I ASK YOU A FEW QUESTIONS?

If you want more information about conducting this kind of research, you'll find another book in this series, *Successful Market Research In A Week*, helpful. Remember yesterday's task on asking questions: the better the question, the better the answer.

The internet

The internet is a great source of market intelligence and marvellous for finding answers to questions. Locate discussion forums, blogs and websites that focus on customer complaints. You'll be amazed at the sort of complaints customers will talk about on the web.

Forums

Take some time to find and join discussion forums for your market and see what your people are saying. That in itself is an education because you'll read 'the good, the bad and the ugly' about your marketplace, which will give you a real insight into how your market really thinks.

You'll even see some questions asked that you can answer in your own business. If the same questions come up time and again, there lies an opportunity. If they're asking, they may not be receiving. There is a gap in the market.

Blogs

Industry blogs and blogs relating to your products or services are other places worth visiting. The really good blog sites share some great information, which can be invaluable. People comment on posts, they ask questions, they get answers in many cases; plus they get solutions. This is a goldmine for 'realtime' intelligence, which you can use to your advantage.

Consumer complaint websites

These websites are another goldmine of information for finding not only the answers to the questions you already have but also even more questions to answer. You can feel the frustration in the comments made, you can hear the customer crying out for solutions and you can harvest a wealth of answers to the questions you've been struggling to answer.

Bonus source

You can set up alerts to notify you when a certain topic is raised on the internet. For example, if you have a gmail account, you can set a feature that lets you know each time a certain phrase or word is mentioned on the web. You'll be alerted and the snippet of it will be emailed straight to your inbox.

Many services and programs are available that allow you to do this, and they are often free. The information you get is invaluable: you get what the market is saying, thinking, liking or disapproving of instantaneously. This gives you an immediate advantage if you can interpret the information correctly.

Other people

If you still have unanswered questions after looking up off-the-shelf information, talking to your customers and searching the internet, there are a few other people you can talk to.

Suppliers

Your suppliers can give you plenty of information about your raw materials and other supplies. They are also often experts in their own field, which could be very useful to you.

They can tell you something about what your competitors are up to if they also supply them. Don't expect them to give away any confidences, though; you wouldn't want them to tell your competitors confidential information about you. But they can probably tell you, for example, whether you get more or fewer complaints relating to their supplies.

Competitors

While you obviously would not expect access to their confidential customer records, you can find out a good deal about your competitors by visiting them at their shop or exhibition display stand and picking up a brochure. You could also request their sales material through their press advertisements or website.

Phone or email them and ask them to send you a copy of their annual report. If your address gives you away, use a different one. This may seem unethical, but it's normal business practice – you're only asking for publicly available material. And they're probably doing the same thing to you if they have any sense. Make a note of how fast they answer your call and send you their material, and what their attitude is like on the phone.

Non-competing businesses

You can offer to swap useful information with other businesses that sell to the same market. For example, if you sell display stands to shops, talk to someone who sells tills. You both have the same customers. If your business is local, you could phone someone running exactly the same type of business 250 miles away, and offer to swap research information.

Advisors

Take all the advice you can, from bank managers and accountants to your local chamber of commerce. Many of them are experts and can tell you a lot of what you need to know.

Filling in the blanks

You should by now have answered virtually all the questions on your original list. However, if a few questions remain that you don't have answers for, you will have to make an educated guess. At least now you have probably reached the stage where it will be a pretty informed guess. Make it clear that it's a guess by writing something like 'estimate' after it in brackets. That will stop you forgetting later that your answer may not be totally accurate. You must also make yourself a note to find out the accurate answer as soon as you can.

Researching under time or budget limitations

Ideally, always allow yourself a few weeks at least to put together a marketing plan. The work is likely to take a solid week or two, but it will probably need to be spread over several weeks.

However, if you've just picked this book up because you have to produce a marketing plan by the end of the month, you probably don't want to hear this. If this is the case, you'll have to put the time available into answering the questions that fall into one of two categories:

● questions that are very important
● questions to which you can't even hazard an answer.

If your business is new, change your schedule to give yourself time to put together the fullest possible marketing plan – it's that important. If you are producing a marketing plan for an existing business, you may find that there are a few things that it will take you a while to establish or that cost more to find out quickly than you can afford. In this case make a good guess and then start researching the answer so you can fill it in accurately as soon as possible.

Suppose you assume that your fast delivery time is important to your customers. Write that down for the time being (noting that it is 'to be confirmed'), and then start asking each customer you deal with whenever you get the chance. In a short while you'll have enough researched answers to be able to fill in the answer properly.

You can schedule in some time in a couple of months for doing fuller research on the other areas that need answers. Put aside time for making phone calls or drawing up a questionnaire.

Summary

By now you should have down most, if not all, of the answers to the questions you created on Monday, using a wide range of sources. These sources should give you all the information you need to put together the marketing plan.

If there are some questions you cannot find the answers to immediately, you'll need to come back to them at a later date and make an educated guess for now. There will be times when an estimate is your best option.

However, with the information you have gathered today, you will have some well-researched and accurate answers by using four main sources of information:

- off-the-shelf information

- customers

- the internet

- other people.

SUNDAY

MONDAY

TUESDAY

WEDNESDAY

THURSDAY

FRIDAY

SATURDAY

Fact-check [answers at the back]

1. What are the four main sources of answers to research questions?
   a) Newsagent, supermarket, department store, cinema ❏
   b) Leisure centre, airport, train station, police station ❏
   c) Off the shelf, customers, the internet, other people ❏
   d) Family, friends, colleagues, the boss ❏

2. What can a library offer to help your research?
   a) Directories listing potential customers, competitors, products and industries ❏
   b) Information about trade associations or societies ❏
   c) Marketing information and market research reports ❏
   d) All of the above ❏

3. How can trade associations and regulatory bodies help you?
   a) They publish annual reports and industry information ❏
   b) They tell you who your competitors are ❏
   c) They can lend you money ❏
   d) They can give you publicity ❏

4. How can trade publications help you?
   a) They are packed with useful information ❏
   b) They are a handy last resort ❏
   c) They look good in your office ❏
   d) They show colleagues that you are on top of things ❏

5. What useful information do government departments provide?
   a) Census reports ❏
   b) Overseas trade information ❏
   c) Data on social trends ❏
   d) All of the above ❏

6. What help can your local enterprise agency offer?
   a) Advice and support to businesses ❏
   b) Financial help ❏
   c) Information about grants and loans ❏
   d) Free office space ❏

7. What are two methods of asking your customers questions?
   a) Discussion forum ❏
   b) Fax ❏
   c) Face to face ❏
   d) Phone call ❏

8. How can you get answers to your questions from the internet?
   a) Through competitors' websites ❏
   b) Through blogs ❏
   c) Through discussion forums ❏
   d) All of the above ❏

9. What type of internet feature can alert you to up-to-date information on a keyword or phrase?
   a) Autoresponder ❏
   b) Instant Chat ❏
   c) Email alerts ❏
   d) SMS text messages ❏

10. If you still have unanswered questions, what else can you do?

a) See a counsellor ☐
b) Speak with other people ☐
c) Consult relevant websites ☐
d) Consult a dictionary ☐

WEDNESDAY

Finding your objectives

Today we will look at what many people regard as the heart of the marketing plan. In fact, the rest is just as crucial, but it's true that this section gives you direction and tells you where you should focus. Once the plan is complete, this is the part that helps you keep your eye on the ball.

You have spent the last couple of days establishing where you are now. So it's time to consider where you are going with your business. That's what we'll be doing today. There are three stages in this process:

1 Identify your critical success factors.
2 Set your objectives.
3 Draw up your sales forecast.

You've already made things considerably easier for yourself by working out where you are now, so don't be daunted by phrases like 'critical success factors' and 'sales forecast'. It's really not difficult, as we're about to find out.

Your critical success factors

These are the things you absolutely *must* do well in order for your business to succeed. They are your priorities and come under categories such as:

- reducing costs
- improving customer service
- speeding up lead times or delivery times
- developing new products
- improving quality
- increasing the size of your customer base
- improving after-sales service.

- product testing

These are just a few of the broad categories in which you might have to improve your performance. The improvements you need to make in your own situation will probably be narrower and more specific than this. For example, when it comes to reducing costs, critical to your success will probably be fairly precise factors such as reducing delivery or sales costs.

Use your competitor comparison table

How do you identify your own critical success factors? Today you'll find that you can only decide where you are going by referring to the work you've done already. And that process starts here.

On Monday we drew up a table comparing your product and service with your main competitors', which you should have filled in by now. You'll need to refer to this table in order to work out your critical success factors.

When you study the table, you'll see where your performance is falling significantly below that of your competitors. You'll also see where everyone is scoring high or performing well; these are usually the areas that are crucial in your line of business. Perhaps everyone's prices are low, or everyone repairs faults within four hours. Have a look at this sample section from the table.

Competitor comparison table

	Your product or service	Competitor 1	Competitor 2
Delivery	8	6	7
After-sales service	3	4	2
Quality	4	7	8

Everybody is clearly putting a high priority on delivery, and you compare well with the competition. Your after-sales service is poor, but so is everyone else's. Perhaps this isn't too important to your customers. When it comes to quality, however, your marks are below the rest of the opposition's. They are giving it high priority – they presumably think it's important – but you don't seem to be competing well at all.

This suggests that quality is a critical success factor that you need to work on. It suggests that delivery is also one of your critical success factors, but in this case one where you are doing well.

Double-check your facts

You can't rely on this table alone. But that's okay. You've done enough work already so that you don't have to. For one thing, you might know something the table doesn't – perhaps you have a successful strategy of operating at a low quality and therefore a lower price than anyone else. If you know this strategy works, it overrides anything the table is telling you.

You can also check this information against your customer research, from your sales records as well as from talking to customers or reading other people's research. It should confirm whether or not quality is a critical factor. It should also tell you whether delivery is as important to your customers as you and your competitors seem to think. And are you all correct in thinking that after-sales service isn't important? Perhaps this is one area where you can get ahead of the field.

More often than not, your other research will bear out your competitor comparison table. But sometimes there will be differences, so it's always important to double-check.

List your critical success factors

Remember that you're focusing on your *critical* factors at the moment. This means looking particularly at the areas you rely on to keep your competitive edge rather than at all the ones where there's scope for improvement. Make a new list of these critical factors, because you'll need them in order to set your objectives.

If you're just starting out in business, you can work out the critical factors by looking at your competitors' performance alone. You still go through this process, but you leave your own performance out of the equation for now.

Your objectives

These are your statements of what you are aiming to achieve. Clearly, the critical success factors you have just listed will be top priority. These are not optional, by definition. If a factor is critical to your success, you must address it. Otherwise you can't succeed.

After that, you can go through the rest of the facts you have collected and establish what other objectives to set yourself.

- The answers to your questions about your **products or services** may highlight areas where you need to make improvements, such as sourcing raw materials or packaging design.
- The information about your **customers** should tell you whether you are missing openings in the market that you should explore, or whether there are aspects of your product design that your customers would like to see improved.
- The information about your **competitors** – other than the table we've just looked at – will tell you which factors, while not actually critical to success, nevertheless leave room for improvement. Perhaps they have a cheaper source of raw materials than you, or lower labour costs, enabling them to keep prices down.
- And your **SWOT analysis** will identify your business strengths and opportunities to exploit and weaknesses and threats to overcome.

Set your timescale

How far ahead are these objectives supposed to be set? Are we talking next week's plans or next year's? It varies from one business to the next, but generally speaking you should be looking a year ahead. In some businesses it will need to be longer. For example, if you build and sell cruise liners that take years to build, you should be looking much further ahead.

Start with a one-year plan, unless there's an obvious reason not to, and revise this later if necessary. You will be reviewing your plan regularly, as we'll see on Saturday, and every so often it will need a full update.

If you have a slack period in the year, this is a good time to hold a regular update. This means that, just before your annual update, your plan won't be looking very far ahead at all. If you need to work a year ahead all the time, update every couple of months so that you have a constantly rolling marketing plan.

How to express your objectives

While you need to be realistic with your objectives, you also need to challenge yourself. Make sure that you are as specific as possible about what you're going to achieve. For example, suppose your delivery isn't as fast as the competition's. You need to improve it. Your objective should not simply state, 'To speed up delivery'. You need to say exactly what you will aim for: 'To deliver 95 per cent of orders within four working hours, and the remainder within six hours'.

Set your priorities

Some of your objectives can be achieved without investment. But some cannot, and you won't necessarily be able to afford to make all the necessary investments straight away. So you need to prioritize.

We've already seen that the objectives related to your critical success factors have to be addressed at once. But what do you do about the rest of them?

Not all your objectives will relate directly to your products or services, but many of them will. If you have a fairly broad product range, you may need to decide which products to invest in first. If you get this right, you should realize a sufficient return on investment to be able to fund the next phase of objectives.

The simple matrix shown below can help you work out which of your products or services are most worth while.

Priorities matrix

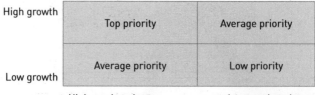

Allocate each of your products or services to one of these categories, according to its growth rate and its share of the market. If your company is local, this means your share of the local market for the product. As you can see, top priority should go to fast-growing products with a high share of the market.

As far as your priorities for your other objectives are concerned, estimate for each one the cost of achieving it and the potential revenue as a result of achieving it. Then grade them according to their potential profit (i.e. revenue minus cost). If you need to estimate the potential revenue you could gain by improving, say, an aspect of your after-sales service, do this on the basis of the extra sales it will earn you (or the value of the customers you now lose that you won't once the improvement is made).

Your sales forecast

The purpose of the sales forecast is not to set yourself impossible tasks. You are supposed to be forecasting what you expect your sales to be, not what you would like them to be.

There will inevitably be more guesswork involved if you are starting up a business than if you have last year's sales figures to go on, but the principles are essentially the same.

To help you estimate what your sales will be, you need to consider several factors. You should by now have found out pretty much everything you can about the following influences on your sales.

● **The market**
- Are you selling into a growing or shrinking market?
- Do you know what the market trends are?
- Are there opportunities or threats that are likely to affect your sales?

● **The products or services**
- Do your products and services have a natural shelf life?
- Are you planning new products?
- Are you aiming to introduce existing products to a wider market?

● **The competition**
- What are your competitors up to?
- Are you likely to be competing harder for your share of the market, or will it get easier if, say, a main competitor has gone out of business?
- Are you going to have to offer greater discounts or take on more staff in order to hold on to your share of the market?

● **The customers**
- Are any of your large customers growing or likely to increase their business with you?
- Are any of them in danger of going bust or moving away?

● **Contract payments**
- Do you have regular large contracts with regular payments?
- Are you expecting to win – or lose – any large contracts in the next year?

● **Seasonal patterns**
- Do your sales fluctuate through the year? (If you sell beachwear, for example, your sales will be lower in November than in June.)

Drawing up the forecast

Once you've gathered all your information, it isn't difficult to estimate what your sales are likely to be over the next year. The important thing is that you should register a profit. If you don't, it's no good tweaking the figures. You will have to adjust your entire operation until the forecast shows that you will be in profit.

The only exception to this is if you are just starting up in business, when it will probably be necessary to operate at a loss for a while until sales have built up. In this case, forecast up to the point where you start to show a consistent profit, even if you do have to put the last few months in pencil.

Weekly or monthly?

Most businesses forecast monthly sales, and find this sufficient. But if you're in a fast-moving market, where you have to respond quickly to new trends, you may need to forecast on a weekly basis. If you only find out once a month whether you're on target, you might have lost valuable time learning that you're behind target – time that you could have spent making changes.

What does a sales forecast look like?

A sales forecast can be just about as simple or as fancy as you like. To begin with a simple version, all you do is draw up a table with the next 12 months (or 52 weeks) across the top. Down the side you list each of your products or services.

Now you simply fill in each square with the amount of sales revenue you expect from each product in that month. As you can see from the following example, this allows you to add up rows or columns to calculate the total sales revenue for each month, or the total revenue from each product or service over the year.

The example shows the basic format, but some businesses find it helpful to add other things, so add them in if you think they would be useful for you, or add another table to show them.

Product	Month												Total
	1	2	3	4	5	6	7	8	9	10	11	12	
A													
B													
C													
D													
E													
F													
G													
H													
Total income													

Additional information for sales forecasts

- The number of units of each product you expect to sell
- At what (average) price you expect to sell each unit
- Income earned and cash due as separate entries, especially where payment may be slow or delayed
- Sales of each product to each customer type, where you are selling into more than one market
- Sales by geographical location

For sales by product, location or anything other than month or week, it's best to draw up a separate forecast for each month. You can view this alongside your overall basic forecast for the year.

Summary

Today we made real progress towards creating a marketing plan. You know where you are right now and, even more vitally, have set your objectives based on your critical success factors.

The important issue now is to determine what needs to be in place and enabled, focusing on the things that are absolutely essential to your current and future success. Then it's a matter of knowing where you are going. So set yourself challenges, but make them realistic ones, and draw up your sales forecast, based on what you expect your sales to be and not on fantasy.

Once you've carried out all the steps outlined today, you'll be ready to go to the last and final stage. This is working out how to get from where you are now to where you want to be. This involves understanding the steps you have to take to get to there. You have to work through, solve or find answers to various problems, all of which will help deliver you to your objectives.

SUNDAY
MONDAY
TUESDAY
WEDNESDAY
THURSDAY
FRIDAY
SATURDAY

Fact-check [answers at the back]

1. How many stages are there to consider when you analyse where you are going with your business?
   a) Four ❏
   b) Six ❏
   c) Three ❏
   d) Five ❏

2. When it comes to your marketing plan, what do critical success factors mean?
   a) Things you absolutely *must* do well in order for your business to be successful ❏
   b) Things that are urgent but not important ❏
   c) Things you can leave till later ❏
   d) Things your competitors do better than you ❏

3. Why is it a good idea to double-check your facts?
   a) Because you can't rely on your competitor comparison table alone ❏
   b) Because you may find different results from other research ❏
   c) Because your competitors' assumptions about the market may not be correct ❏
   d) All of the above ❏

4. What are the three main stages of planning where you are going with your business?
   a) Design your logo, order stationery, hire staff ❏
   b) Identify critical success factors, set objectives, draw up your sales forecast ❏
   c) Look at your competitors, borrow money, talk to customers ❏
   d) Keep prices down, speed up delivery, improve after-sales service ❏

5. Generally, how far ahead should you be looking when planning?
   a) Two weeks ❏
   b) A year ❏
   c) Three months ❏
   d) Six months ❏

6. What can help you work out which of your products or services are most worth while?
   a) A simple matrix ❏
   b) A crystal ball ❏
   c) Past pricing policies ❏
   d) A sales forecast ❏

7. What is a sales forecast designed to tell you?
   a) What you would like your sales to be ❏
   b) What you expect your sales to be ❏
   c) What the market trends are ❏
   d) What the competition is up to ❏

8. How many factors should
   you consider to help you
   estimate what your sales
   will be?
a) None ❑
b) One ❑
c) Two ❑
d) Several ❑

9. What information does a
   sales forecast show?
a) Seasonal patterns ❑
b) Total sales revenue for
   each month ❑
c) Total revenue for the year ❑
d) All of the above ❑

10. What additional information
    could you include in a sales
    forecast?
a) Expected sales by product ❑
b) Expected sales by location ❑
c) Past sales by product ❑
d) Past sales by location ❑

THURSDAY

Converting your objectives into action plans

The final stage of preparation, before you finally commit your plan to paper, is to work out how you're going to get from where you are to where you're going – your route map. There are three steps you have to go through to convert each of your objectives (from yesterday) into a strategy, or action plan:

1 Look at the options.
2 Consider the practicalities.
3 Select the best route.

Now that you have your list of objectives, you will need to go through them in turn to put together a mini action plan for each one. When you've finished, all these action plans together will make up your marketing strategy.

You've already established that your objectives are achievable – if challenging – so you know it's all possible. Every one of your objectives can generate a workable action plan. Today we will look at the best way to do it.

Look at the options

For most of the objectives you have set, you'll find that there are a number of ways to achieve them; in other words, you have a number of options. Start by taking each objective separately, going through the process outlined in this chapter to discover the possible routes for getting from point A to point B.

Let's take the example that you're trying to reduce your delivery times to less than four working hours. There are several (feasible) ways you might do this. You might consider:

● contracting out all your deliveries to someone else
● changing your working system so that orders are processed faster and drivers check in more frequently
● employing more drivers.

You might well come up with more options if you're in this situation. For the moment, simply write down the possibilities. We'll discuss how to pick the right one in a minute.

The important thing is to think as freely as possible to make sure you consider everything that might be useful. This is a process in which imaginative thinking and an open-minded approach are valuable. Try to brainstorm ideas for this with other people if you can; it's an excellent way to generate ideas.

There are more methods than can possibly be listed here for improving every aspect of your marketing. But it is possible to give you an idea of the kinds of activities to think about. These can be broadly divided into five main marketing areas, as shown in the following box. Most of your objectives will fall into one of these categories.

Five key areas of marketing

1 Increase awareness of your company and your products or services.

2 Increase existing customers' loyalty.

3 Secure sales.

4 Generate higher turnover.

5 Increase your knowledge of your market.

We can take each of these in turn and list the type of options you should be considering. However, don't be tempted to think that these lists are exhaustive. Be open to thinking up other approaches for achieving your objectives as well.

1 Increase awareness of your company

- Advertising – local and national press, trade press, radio, TV *runners Magazines?*
- Press releases – in the local, national or trade press, online
- Direct mail – using your own mailing list, bought list, rented lists
- Exhibitions
- Internet
- Sales promotions
- Telephone selling
- Personal sales visits
- Customer/prospect newsletter
- Special events
- Sponsorship

2 Increase customer loyalty

- Improve customer care
- Make more contacts with customers
- Give customers a single point of contact
- Improve delivery
- Improve product quality
- Improve after-sales service
- Improve accuracy of billing

3 Secure sales

- Close the sale on a higher percentage of visits/phone calls
- Improve quality/range of brochures and other sales literature
- Get customer's signature on contract/deposit earlier in process
- Improve sales training for staff

4 Generate higher turnover

- Increase sales on certain products and services
- Launch new products and services
- Increase prices
- Concentrate on the most profitable product lines
- Employ more sales staff
- Use sales agents
- Open new branches
- Enter new markets
- Sell regionally as well as locally, or nationally as well as regionally
- Start exporting, or expand your exporting operations

5 Increase your market knowledge

- Run customer surveys
- Hold customer forums
- Subscribe to trade journals
- Conduct your own research
- Commission market research
- Buy in ready-made research
- Contribute to online discussion forums
- Talk to suppliers
- Research competitors
- Form partnerships with non-competing businesses

Not every one of these approaches will work for every option, but you will usually find there's more than one way to achieve your objectives.

Make it more specific

These are only broad approaches, of course. They are not the whole story: each of the above points still begs several questions that need answering. Let's look at a few examples.

Increase awareness through exhibitions

This is one way to increase awareness of your company and brand, but your objective will have been more specific. It will have said, for example, 'To increase awareness of our products among business customers in the tourism industry'. Your options for achieving it must be more specific and detailed too. You'll need to suggest which exhibitions you should attend, what stand you should use, which staff should attend and so on.

Increase loyalty by making more contacts with customers

Consider the method – whether to do this by post, email, phone or face to face – and the frequency. You will also need to be clear about your specific purpose in increasing customer loyalty.

Secure sales by improving staff training

You'll need to specify which staff, how much training and in what area. Will you arrange in-house or external training?

Increase market knowledge by commissioning research

This will increase your market knowledge, but, again, you'll need to be more specific. Think about what sort of research you will commission. Will it be in the form of questionnaires, in the post or online, or people with clipboards on street corners? Who do you intend to survey? What sort of information are you aiming to get from it? From whom will you commission the research?

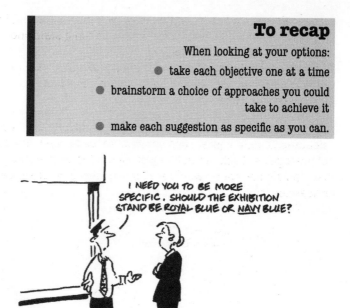

Consider the practicalities

Now that you have a list of objectives, each with a choice of ways to achieve it, you need to start finding out which approach is best in each case. The way to do this is to examine the implications of each option from a practical point of view.

In each case you need to calculate:

● **the potential revenue** from achieving the objective using this method

● **the cost** of using this method

● **the time implications** – how long it will take to achieve it and when you could start – in other words, what the schedule would be

● **the staffing implications** – whether it could be done by existing staff, or whether you need to bring in experienced people or contract out. (This obviously has an impact on your costs as well.)

- **the training** needed to put this approach into operation, how long it will take and whether you have suitable staff who could be trained up effectively
- **the transport implications** – whether you would have to commit to more deliveries, start shipping overseas or increase your fleet size.

You should have enough information to be able to do these calculations quite easily. Then you'll be ready to weigh up the options against each other. If any of your calculations show that a particular option won't be cost-effective, either revise it or abandon it.

Select the best route

By the time you've identified all the feasible options and then considered the practical implications of each one, you should find that it's not difficult to choose the best way to meet your objectives. If you find that there isn't much to choose between two or more of the options, don't waste time deciding which option to take. If either will do the job equally well, pick either; it probably doesn't matter which you choose.

There is one thing, however, that you must consider: combining options. This often results in the best of all worlds. Take our example of reducing delivery times to less than four working hours. We identified three basic options for doing this:

- contracting out all your deliveries to someone else
- changing your working system so that orders are processed faster and drivers check in more frequently
- employing more drivers.

These options are not mutually exclusive. Once you've weighed up the practicalities, consider mixing some of the options. For example, you could:

- change your working system, but *also* contract out some deliveries at peak times
- change your system *and* employ a part-time driver from 2 p.m. to 4 p.m. each afternoon.

Mixing several approaches
When it comes to objectives that relate to increasing awareness of your company, or your products or services, you'll find that several approaches will often work. They can frequently be mixed and will often support each other to give you a better result than they ever could alone.

Other examples of combining two or more approaches to give better results than one could on its own include:

- combining direct mailshots with telephone selling
- supporting an appearance at an exhibition with advertising in the trade press
- running several awareness campaigns independently of one another, such as:
  - a feature in the local paper
  - articles for online directories
  - a trade exhibition
  - a telemarketing campaign.

This last approach would be particularly suitable if you need to increase awareness in several distinct markets. You could also target social networking sites and share what you have to offer.

Budgeting

Once you have decided which options to choose, it should be fairly straightforward to calculate the cost of meeting each objective – you've already costed each option, after all.

All you have to do is add up the individual costs of meeting each of the objectives and you have your overall marketing budget. You already know how much revenue you expect it to generate and that it will more than pay for itself.

It will sometimes happen, nevertheless, that you simply can't afford to invest this much at once, until you've started to see some return. In this case you will need to go back and revise the options.

If you can't reduce the costs, put some of the lower-priority objectives on hold until the increased revenue from the first few is available to pay for them. In this case, budget in this revenue, and also show in your budget that you will be reinvesting the revenue once you have it – later in the year – to put your other strategies into practice.

Your finished action plan

At the end of all this you will have a clear list of objectives, and you will have drawn up your action plan for meeting each one. This should not only outline how you will meet each objective but also give you a schedule for doing so.

Summary

Today you've gone through the process of converting your objectives into a workable marketing strategy or action plan. You took the steps needed to work out how you're going to get from where you are to where you want to be.

Now that you know all the options available to you, you can put to work the five key areas of marketing to your advantage and move towards each of your targeted objectives. You can use a wide range of tools to increase awareness of your company. Whichever ones you decide on will need to move you effectively and profitably to your end result.

When you have taken into account the practicalities, you can choose the best route based on this information. Some areas will be challenging and at times frustrating, especially if you don't have all the information you need, and taking an educated guess will have to do.

However, if you followed the path laid out for you over the past few days, you'll be well on your way to having a marketing plan to be proud of. More importantly, it will be a key tool for achieving your desired result.

SUNDAY

MONDAY

TUESDAY

WEDNESDAY

THURSDAY

FRIDAY

SATURDAY

Fact-check [answers at the back]

1. How many steps must you take to convert each of your objectives into a marketing strategy or action plan?
   a) One ❏
   b) Two ❏
   c) Three ❏
   d) Four ❏

2. What are two of the key aims of marketing?
   a) To increase existing customers' loyalty ❏
   b) To increase knowledge of the competition ❏
   c) To secure sales ❏
   d) To employ more sales staff ❏

3. How could you increase awareness of your company's products or services?
   a) Through advertising ❏
   b) Through press releases ❏
   c) By employing more staff ❏
   d) All of the above ❏

4. When looking at your options, what should you do?
   a) Take each objective one at a time ❏
   b) Brainstorm your choice of approach ❏
   c) Make each suggestion as specific as possible ❏
   d) All of the above ❏

5. Why do you need to consider each option from a practical point of view?
   a) To understand the cost implications ❏
   b) To understand the time implications ❏
   c) To calculate your marketing budget ❏
   d) All of the above ❏

6. How should you choose the best approach to achieving an objective?
   a) Examine the implications from a practical point of view ❏
   b) See which one is the least expensive ❏
   c) Consult your investors ❏
   d) Ensure that no extra staff training is needed ❏

7. Why is it a good idea to combine two or more approaches to marketing?
   a) They can give better results than one approach alone ❏
   b) It saves money ❏
   c) It saves time ❏
   d) It saves effort ❏

8. Why should you look at each option from a budgetary point of view?
   a) To identify lower-priority objectives ❏
   b) To see if you can afford it ❏
   c) To calculate revenue ❏
   d) To give you a schedule ❏

9. If you can't reduce the costs, what should you do?
a) Keep your options as a high priority ❏
b) Abandon the marketing plan ❏
c) Revise the marketing plan ❏
d) Go ahead anyway ❏

10. What should your action plan include?
a) An outline of how you will meet your objectives ❏
b) Your sales forecast ❏
c) A schedule for meeting your objectives ❏
d) A SWOT analysis ❏

FRIDAY

Putting the plan together

Congratulations: you've done all the thinking work. Now you simply have to put your plan down on paper with everything in the right order. This is a fairly straightforward process, which will get you from the huge pile of material you have assembled to a few smartly presented pages that are easy to understand.

Today we will go through the steps involved in putting the plan together. These are the steps:

1 Assemble your data.
2 Review the plan as a whole.
3 Establish the content.
4 Plan the design and layout.
5 Write it up clearly and simply.

The aim is to end up with a document that you can work from efficiently and that you would be proud to show your bank or any other outsider who needed to see it.

Assemble your data

The first thing you need to do is to collect together all the finalized information for your marketing plan. You don't need to include the books and documents you used to research it, or the lists of notes: you just need the results of your research, which will be as follows:

- answers to the questions we asked on Monday
- competitor comparison table
- SWOT analysis
- objectives
- sales forecast
- marketing strategy.

Keep the rest of your notes and research data – survey results or whatever – in a safe place. You never know when you might want to refer back to them.

Review the plan as a whole

This is your chance to go through all this final material in one go, so that you review the plan as a whole rather than looking at it in bits, as you have done up to now.

Look through the material still on your desk. It's a good idea to do this after you've had a break from the detailed work of planning the strategy. The following morning is a good time for it.

The aim is to give yourself an overview of the whole thing, because you may find when you do this that a couple of items don't quite work or fit together. For example, something important in the early research may have somehow failed to make its way into the objectives or strategy, or you may now feel that you can answer an important question that you were unable to earlier.

Establish the content

The next step is to work out what is going to go into the final plan. You may feel disappointed about leaving out things that you spent a long time working on, but this work is not wasted. For one thing, you needed to do the work in order to arrive at a really effective plan. For another, you can keep the material for reference and – as you'll see tomorrow – there'll be plenty of opportunities to refer back.

You may also find that interested parties such as the bank or the shareholders may want more background detail on certain aspects of the plan. That's when you'll be able to produce all that extra material that never made it into the final document.

So what is going to find its way into the final plan? Some things are compulsory and some are optional. There is a list of things that really have to be there; everyone expects it. The following table shows the content that should always be included in the finished plan.

However, that doesn't mean that everything else is banned. Although you will want to keep the document as brief as possible – ideally 10–25 pages – if there's other information you feel is particularly important, you can include it.

Core contents of the marketing plan

1 Where your business is now	● Key facts about your products or services ● Key facts about the customers ● Key facts about the competition (including the comparison table) ● SWOT analysis
2 Where your business is going	● Your objectives ● Your sales forecast
3 How your business is going to get there	● Your marketing strategy

You'll notice that you need to include only the key facts about your products or services, your customers and your competitors. Only you will know precisely what these are.

The point is that, once you've answered some of your early questions, you'll find that some of the answers repeat each other, and some of the information turns out – once you have it – to be less relevant than it might have been. So you won't necessarily need to reproduce the full list of answers that you researched.

You should be able to judge this for yourself and, if in doubt, keep the information in there. You can always put it in an appendix at the back so it's not in the way for anyone who doesn't need to read it.

You'll need to organize the core contents of the marketing plan into a broader structure that makes the whole thing easier to read and to use. This structure is shown in the table below.

Structure of the marketing plan

Cover page	Include company name, address, phone number and the date the plan was prepared; also give your own name and phone number
Contents page	List the main headings of the document and those within the core content
Summary	This is a brief précis of what's in the document
The core content	See the previous table
Appendices	Add them if you think it would help to include your extra information here

The first three of these – cover page, contents page and summary – should go at the beginning, in that order. The summary is extremely important. It may not matter much to you – you know what's in the document anyway – but, if you have to show your marketing plan to the bank or other potential investors, they may well decide whether or not to read the whole plan purely on the basis of the summary.

The summary

The summary should contain everything that is in the main part of the document, but in brief. It should list the results of key points from each section:

● **Where you are now**
  - a brief description of the products, type of customers and key competitors
  - the most crucial one or two strengths and opportunities

TIP

Summarize your strengths
Since the summary is usually for people who, you hope, will invest in your business, don't call attention to your weaknesses at this point. They need to be included in the plan – it wouldn't be credible without them, and a smart investor will spot them anyway – but they don't need to go into the summary.

- **Where you are going**
  - your key objectives
  - the bottom line of the sales forecast (but not the monthly or weekly breakdown)

- **How you are going to get there**
  - your strategy summarized, but without the detailed specification of each action point

Leave out the details

When summarizing your strategy, just mention the first stage you went through. You can say, for example, that you will 'increase your customer base by 30 per cent through advertising and exhibitions' without giving details of which exhibitions you plan to attend.

The point of the summary is to give a brief précis, so keep it short. Aim to keep it to one page unless the whole document is long, in which case you may have to run over to a second page.

Although the summary goes at the beginning, you will no doubt have realized for yourself that the sensible thing is to write it last. If you do this, you'll find it far quicker and easier to do. You'll probably find it a helpful mental exercise as well. It tends to focus the mind on the absolutely central issues in a way that can give you a much clearer vision of where you're leading your business.

Plan the design and layout

We've already seen that the finished document should be 10–25 pages long, depending on the size of your business. This may seem rather long, but if you want to impress people with your plan, you will need to present it professionally and clearly, and that takes up more space than presenting it badly. You could cram the plan into four or five pages, but it would look impenetrable and be hard to read.

Let's take a look at the most important rules of layout and presentation for creating a smart, professional document.

Consider the packaging

The first thing to consider is the packaging. You don't want to present someone with a few pieces of paper stapled together and tell them it's your marketing plan. At the other extreme, you don't need to have it leather bound with your company name engraved on the cover in gold leaf. Apart from anything else, this gives the impression that the contents are likewise engraved – in stone. A marketing plan is a flexible document and it should give that impression.

By far the best approach is to use a good-quality laser or inkjet printer, and print out your plan on good-quality, plain white paper (not laid paper, which is the finely textured paper often used for letterheads – it doesn't take print so well).

Then have the whole thing bound with, for instance, a spiral binding and a clear plastic cover front and back. That will look smart and professional but not over the top.

Give it space

Your marketing plan will look much better, and be easier for you and anyone else to read and use, if you use double spacing and reasonably wide margins. It will look more professional if you justify the text (in other words, line up the right-hand ends of the lines). This will also help focus the eye on the text, which makes it look more important.

Make it easy to follow

Having included a contents list, you will naturally number the pages to help other people find their way around the plan. You will also need to include clear headings and sub-headings to make sure the reader can find the section they are looking for. This has the added benefit of breaking the text up a little more so that it looks readable and approachable.

Keep it simple

Limit yourself to two fonts (types of lettering) for the whole document. Use one for headings and one for text, or stick to just one throughout if you like. You can use different sizes, bold, italics and so on, but in moderation.

The aim is to produce a document that is clean, readable and easy to follow. You're supposed to be exercising your marketing skills, not your prowess as a designer. Fussy or fancy designs distract the reader from the content, which is the part that matters in a marketing plan.

Make sure any tables, such as the sales forecast or competitor comparison table, are neat and simple. A page of text that includes tables or charts may look confusing and messy if the graphics are at all fussy.

Don't play around with masses of different line thicknesses and typefaces. Just use bold type for column and row headings and keep the whole thing as simple as possible.

By the same token, don't start showing off with clever icons or bits of clip art. By all means put your logo on the title page, and perhaps even at the very end if much of the last page is left blank, but leave it at that.

Write it up clearly

Now that you have a smart-looking, well-presented marketing plan that contains all the essential information, the only thing left is to make sure that whoever you show it to can read it.

Guidelines for writing clear English

- Use ordinary, everyday language – don't try to be clever.
- Use short words.
- Use short sentences – average 20 words and don't exceed 40.
- Use short paragraphs – they should never look deeper than they are wide.
- Don't use jargon that your readers might not be familiar with.
- Avoid legal terms and pompous words such as 'herewith' and 'therein'.
- Use active rather than passive verbs – make the subject of the sentence do something rather than have it done to them: e.g. *The boss phoned me* rather than *I was phoned by the boss.*
- Use concrete rather than abstract nouns – abstract nouns often end with '-tion': e.g. write *car* rather than *transportation.*

These are a few guidelines that are worth following to make sure that your style is clear and easy to understand, and that people enjoy reading your plan. If the language is convoluted or over-complicated, it can be so hard to work out what the individual words and sentences mean that it becomes impossible to take in the overall meaning of the document.

Summary

Today you learned about the five stages of piecing your plan together, so that you have all the tools you need to complete the marketing plan on which you've spent so much time and effort.

The first two stages – assembling the data and reviewing the plan as a whole – give you your first proper opportunity to gain an overview of the work you've done up to now. The next three stages – establishing the contents, planning the design and layout, and writing it up – are the process of transferring the work to the final document.

All these steps will help you ensure that you can establish exactly what to include in your marketing plan, and how to structure and present it so that it looks smart and professional but simple and easy to read.

Once you have your completed marketing plan, all that's left is to ensure that you get the most out of it. After all, you want to make all the work that's gone into it worth while – and it will be. Tomorrow we will learn how to use the plan effectively in order to grow your business.

SUNDAY
MONDAY
TUESDAY
WEDNESDAY
THURSDAY
FRIDAY
SATURDAY

Fact-check [answers at the back]

1. Which of these is *not* one of the steps in putting your final plan together?
   a) Assemble your data and review the plan as a whole ❏
   b) Establish the content ❏
   c) Check that your facts are correct and review your sales forecast ❏
   d) Write it up clearly and simply ❏

2. What data do you *not* need to assemble beforehand?
   a) Answers to the questions you asked on Monday ❏
   b) Your company accounts ❏
   c) Your SWOT analysis ❏
   d) Your objectives ❏

3. What content is optional to include in your final plan?
   a) Facts about your products or services ❏
   b) Appendices with extra information ❏
   c) Facts about the customers ❏
   d) Facts about the competition ❏

4. What information has to be included in your final plan?
   a) Where your business is now ❏
   b) Where your business is going ❏
   c) How your business is going to get there ❏
   d) All of the above ❏

5. What should the cover page of your plan include?
   a) Your company name, address and phone number ❏
   b) The date the plan was prepared ❏
   c) Your own name and phone number ❏
   d) All of the above ❏

6. What should you always have to hand when writing up your plan?
   a) A large glass of water ❏
   b) A large whisky ❏
   c) Guidelines for writing clear English ❏
   d) Plenty of good-quality paper ❏

7. What should your marketing plan summary contain?
   a) Key points from each section ❏
   b) A list of events and exhibitions you will attend ❏
   c) Information about the competition ❏
   d) A weekly breakdown of sales ❏

8. How long should your plan be?
   a) One to three pages ❏
   b) Four to five pages ❏
   c) Between 10 and 25 pages ❏
   d) At least 25 pages ❏

9. How can you make your marketing plan easy to follow and simple?
   a) Limit yourself to two fonts ❏
   b) Print it on laid paper ❏
   c) Limit icons and clip art ❏
   d) Have it bound in leather ❏

10. What should you avoid when writing up your plan?
   a) Jargon ❏
   b) Legal terms ❏
   c) Long sentences ❏
   d) All of the above ❏

SATURDAY

Using your marketing plan

You've spent the last few days putting together your marketing plan from scratch, and you should now have a smart document sitting neatly on your desk. Today we shall recap everything we did to get here, before discussing how to use the plan to its maximum effectiveness.

Drawing up a successful marketing plan involves:

- asking the right questions
- researching the answers
- setting the objectives and sales forecast
- planning the marketing strategy
- putting it all together.

It's not a difficult process, but it's taken a fair bit of work and it would be a shame not to put it to the best use possible. So the last thing we're going to do today – but by no means the least important – is to find out what you're supposed to do with the thing now you've got it.

Asking the right questions

On Monday we looked at the first stage of the marketing plan: drawing up a list of questions. The important thing is to ask the right questions so that you collect all the information you're going to need later.

We established that there are four areas you needed to ask questions about:

1 your product or service
2 your customers
3 your competitors
4 your business.

To begin with, you have to specify exactly what it is that you're marketing. If you never focus on this, you'll never notice if it needs to change. We looked at some of the most important questions to ask, as listed in the box below.

Questions about the product or service

- What is the product or service?
- Where do the raw materials come from?
- What is the packaging like?
- How is the product transported?
- Where is it sold?
- In what form does it reach the customer?
- Does it need explaining?
- Is it easy to use?
- How easy is it to increase production if sales go up?

Next, we examined the sort of questions you need to ask about your customers and potential customers. Of course, if you're just starting out in business, all of your customers will be potential.

We discussed the importance of asking yourself uncomfortable questions, such as what your customers dislike about your product. Only by investigating these areas will you really learn what you need to know about how you can keep improving your business.

Questions about the customers

- Who are they?
- What are their buying trends?
- How much will they pay?
- How do they know about the product or service?
- Where do they buy it?
- What do they like about your product or service?
- What do they dislike about it?
- What do they like about this type of product or service?
- What do they dislike about this type of product or service?
- Why do your existing customers choose your product or service rather than your competitors'?

The next area we asked questions about was the competition. You need to check out any other business that your potential customers might go to instead of buying from you. They may not even be selling the same product; it could be a competing type of product. If you sell electric egg whisks, for example, companies selling rotary whisks are competing with you.

Questions about the competition

- Who are your competitors?
- What product or service are your prospects using at the moment?
- Do your competitors offer anything beyond a basic product or service and, if so, what?
- What has each of your competitors got that you haven't?

We also drew up a table of comparison with your competitors. We listed you and your competitors across the top, and the various factors to compare down the side. This gives you an at-a-glance picture of where you are doing well or badly against the rest of the field.

Lastly, we asked questions about the business, which we did using SWOT analysis.

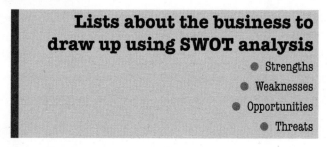

Lists about the business to draw up using SWOT analysis

- Strengths
- Weaknesses
- Opportunities
- Threats

Researching the answers

On Tuesday we researched the answers to all these questions. We found there were four places you could go to find answers:

1 off-the-shelf information
2 your customers and potential customers
3 the internet
4 other people.

Off-the-shelf information	Your customers	The internet	Other people
● Your own records ● Directories and websites ● Trade associations and regulatory bodies ● The trade press ● Government departments ● Your local enterprise agency	● Existing customers ● Potential customers ● Ex-customers	● Websites ● Discussion forums ● Blogs	● Suppliers ● Competitors ● Non-competing businesses ● Advisors

You can get information from customers and other people by talking to them, emailing them, phoning them or writing to them, and we looked at the pros and cons of all these approaches.

Setting the objectives and sales forecast

Once you had collected all your information together, you needed to do something with it. By answering the lists of questions, you established where your business is now. It was then time to work out where it's going.

Identify your critical success factors

Going through the answers you found helped you identify which factors are absolutely vital to your success. These are the things without which your business cannot thrive.

Your competitor comparison table showed you where your performance is falling short of the average. You could also see where everyone, including you, is scoring highly. This identified the areas that are likely to be critical.

The weaknesses and threats in your SWOT analysis were also worth checking through, to see if they bore out any other indicators of where you absolutely must improve your performance. They are not an answer in themselves, because not every weakness is crucial, or even avoidable.

Establish your objectives

Next you had to set yourself objectives based on the areas where you need to improve. Top of the list were your critical success factors. You also looked through your other information to work out what needs to be done.

In general, you were setting yourself objectives for the next year. However, in some cases you may be aiming to achieve a certain thing much faster than that, or to reach a particular objective over several years.

TIP Be specific
Make each objective specific, so you know exactly what you're aiming at. Don't aim to 'speed up delivery'; aim to 'deliver 95 per cent of orders within four working hours, and the remainder within six hours'.

We also looked at how to set priorities if you can't afford either the money or the time to pursue all your objectives straight away.

Draw up your sales forecast

This is a forecast of what you expect your sales to be, not a fantasy of what you'd like them to be. There are half a dozen factors, other than your sales figures for last year, that you should take into account to help you estimate your sales as accurately as possible.

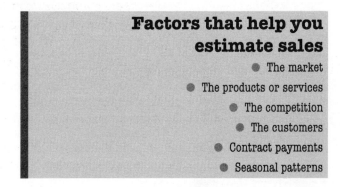

Factors that help you estimate sales
- The market
- The products or services
- The competition
- The customers
- Contract payments
- Seasonal patterns

Planning the marketing strategy

The final stage of preparation involved converting your objectives into action plans. In other words, having established where you are now and where you are going, it was time to establish how you are going to get from A to B. There are three main stages to achieving this:

1 Look at the options.
2 Consider the practicalities.
3 Select the best route.

Look at the options

You need to examine all the plausible options you can think of for achieving each objective. We looked at the kind of approaches you should consider within each of the five main areas of marketing that your objectives are likely to fit into:

● increasing awareness of your company and your products or services
● increasing existing customers' loyalty
● securing sales
● generating higher turnover
● increasing your knowledge of your market.

Examining your options

● Take each objective one at a time.

● Brainstorm a choice of approaches you could take to achieve it.

● Make each suggestion as specific as you can.

Consider the practicalities

The next stage in drawing up your marketing strategy was to look at the practical implications of each option. You needed to consider several aspects:

● potential revenue
● cost
● time implications

● staffing
● training
● transport.

Select the best route

It should be fairly clear which of the options you identified is going to be the most effective. If there's nothing to choose between them, it doesn't matter which you go for. Bear in mind the possibility of combining options; this can work very well. We considered one or two ways in which you could do this.

Finally, we looked at the budgeting for your marketing plan. Once you've added up the costs of all the options you plan to adopt, you have a budget. Sometimes you can't afford to launch into all these marketing schemes straight away, so we looked at what you do if this is the case. By the end of Thursday we had a list of objectives with a costed and scheduled action plan for achieving each one.

Putting it all together

On Friday we pulled everything into a finished document. We started by assembling all the data we were going to put into it, and we then reviewed it all together to make sure there was no repetition or inconsistency. Then we established the precise contents of the final document.

Establish the contents

- Cover page
- Contents page
- Summary
- Where you are now:
  - key facts about your products or services
  - key facts about your customers
  - key facts about your competitors
  - SWOT analysis
- Where you are going:
  - your objectives
  - your sales forecast
- How you are going to get there:
  - your marketing strategy
- Appendices (if you need them)

After that, we looked at the key points of layout and design, including packaging, spacing, page numbering and headings. We established the importance of keeping the design clear and simple. We also looked at the guidelines for writing clear English, using short words, sentences and paragraphs.

Making use of your marketing plan

Now that you have your marketing plan, what are you going to do with it? You're going to wring every last drop of value from it, that's what. And you will be able to derive plenty of benefits from it if you use it wisely.

You've already learned a huge amount by creating it, and you will have come up with strategies you would never have arrived at without it. You also have a professional and thorough document you can show to anyone who needs to see it, from your bank to consultants, investors and incoming directors.

The plan is not just a memento of all your hard work, which you frame and hang on the wall, to look impressive. You might as well put it in the bin! It's a key working document from which you can get huge value.

Implement the plan

For a start, you will need to refer to the plan regularly as you implement the strategies that you have set out in it. Your action plan will include a schedule and a budget, so you should have everything you need to start putting it into practice.

Update the plan

If you let your plan sit gathering dust for five years, it will be virtually useless at the end of that time. If you need it then, you'll have to start again from scratch. This is why it's worth keeping it up to date.

When you first researched the answers to your questions, there were probably a few answers that you couldn't find at the time and had to make an educated guess at. Make yourself an action point to deal with this as soon as you can. Be on the lookout for the information you need, and fill in the answers as you find them.

This is worth doing for two reasons:

- You may have guessed wrong, and the right answers might affect your strategy so you need to know about them in order to keep it up to date.
- If you keep your marketing plan regularly updated, you will never have to go through the work of putting it together from scratch again.

You should also schedule an update session (with action points) every so often. Once a year is enough for many companies but, if your business or market is changing fast, once every six months might be better. Make a point of checking every fact to see whether it needs updating. Your product range may have changed, or a new supplier may have arrived on the market. Most facts may not need altering, but you'll miss something if you don't consciously check.

Take your competitor comparison chart as an example. Have any new competitors arrived on the scene? Has one of your competitors revamped and improved their approach to customer care? Is your competition taking advantage of the opportunities of internet and mobile marketing? Are you still doing as well by comparison with the rest of the field? If not, are you doing better or worse?

Review the plan

You also need to review the plan. Again, once a year is usually sufficient but you might want to do it more frequently. Review it shortly after you have updated it.

If you have achieved the objectives you set out last year, you are going to need a new set of objectives and a new strategy to achieve them. Many businesses take a couple of days out for their directors or senior managers to get together and hammer out next year's plan. But you could set aside a long session every few months if that suits you better.

Your update will tell you about any changes in the market, your customers' attitudes, your product, the competition, your strengths and weaknesses, and so on. These will help you devise a new set of objectives, using the same approach as for the original plan.

Use the plan proactively

Keep using the plan to generate ideas. Look at the SWOT analysis and ask yourself if there's anything else you could be doing to build on your strengths or make the most of opportunities.

When things go wrong, use the plan to tell you why. Suppose you start missing your sales targets. The odds are that you'll be able to work out why if you look through your marketing plan. And you'll be able to find a way to get back on target.

Suppose the reason you're missing your targets is that a new competitor has arrived on the scene. Don't give in – fight! Update your competitor comparison table and use it to help you brainstorm ways to maintain and build your share of the market.

Make it stand out

Marketing is like a polar bear in the desert. It Stands Out! Make sure you use your marketing plan and that your marketing is like that polar bear in the desert.

Summary

Today you revised everything you learned this week about making an effective marketing plan that will stand you in good stead as you implement your marketing strategy. We looked at the importance of updating and reviewing it regularly, so that it becomes an essential part of your business that you refer to constantly.

Above all, you have seen that a marketing plan isn't a tedious document you're obliged to prepare to keep your colleagues and investors happy. It's one of the most useful business tools you'll ever lay your hands on, and the more you learn to use it, the more indispensable you will find it.

SUNDAY

MONDAY

TUESDAY

WEDNESDAY

THURSDAY

FRIDAY

SATURDAY

Fact-check [answers at the back]

1. What are two of the key aspects of drawing up your marketing plan?
   a) Asking the right questions ❏
   b) Researching the answers ❏
   c) Finding new premises ❏
   d) Deciding on the typeface ❏

2. Which areas do you need to ask questions about regarding your marketing plan?
   a) Your product ❏
   b) Your business ❏
   c) Your customers ❏
   d) Your bank balance ❏

3. To know exactly what you're marketing, which specific questions should you ask?
   a) What days of the week should we deliver? ❏
   b) What is the packaging like? ❏
   c) Where is it sold? ❏
   d) Why should we use a local delivery firm? ❏

4. To create an effective plan, what questions should you ask your customers?
   a) Who are they? ❏
   b) Do they listen to the BBC World Service? ❏
   c) How much will they pay? ❏
   d) What do they dislike about your product/service? ❏

5. What does the SWOT analysis tool help you do?
   a) Understand who your competitors are ❏
   b) Forecast buying trends ❏
   c) Identify key areas in your business ❏
   d) Give a list of price options ❏

6. Which are useful sources of information when doing research?
   a) Your customers ❏
   b) Directories ❏
   c) Suppliers ❏
   d) Church ❏

7. What does a comparison table give you?
   a) Information about when your taxes are due ❏
   b) Information about where you're falling short ❏
   c) Critical factors ❏
   d) Information about where you are scoring highly ❏

8. Which key factors will help you estimate your sales?
   a) The market ❏
   b) The bank ❏
   c) Your family ❏
   d) Seasonal patterns ❏

9. What is one of the main stages of converting your objectives to actions?
   a) Get your profit and loss accounts from your accountant ❏
   b) Consider the practicalities ❏
   c) Speed up delivery ❏
   d) Lower your prices ❏

10. What are two reasons for regularly updating your plan?
   a) You may have guessed wrong ❏
   b) So you don't have to keep starting from scratch ❏
   c) So the plan is better than your competitors' ❏
   d) To show what you'd like your sales to be ❏

Surviving in tough times

No business is immune from the significant changes that are occurring in the economic environment at present. What's going to happen? What should we do? To a certain extent, it's anyone's guess. What we can be sure of is that many sectors will see shrinkage in demand, and this is likely to increase the competitive pressures facing businesses. Under these conditions, a business must redouble its focus on its two key groups – customers and competitors.

Here are ten crucial marketing tips that you can use to help your business survive and prosper.

1 Refocus on your customers

During difficult times, customers may be changing in terms of their perceived needs, buying habits and attitudes to value. Marketers must not assume they *know* what customers are thinking, and should use current research to ensure that they have an objective view of the situation. Keep information on customers up to date, so that you can identify the right course of action to meet corporate objectives in a changing environment.

2 Refocus on your competitors

Generally, businesses adopt three broad approaches during difficult trading circumstances. Most commonly, firms use price reductions to stimulate their own customers' demand and to attract competitors' customers. Alternatively, firms may seek to increase the benefits they offer while keeping their prices steady (for example with two-for-one offers or free trial periods). Finally, firms seek to create innovative solutions to customers' perceived needs. The marketer must ensure that information on competitor action is collected and used as part of the strategic decision process. The key is to take the right action at the right time, based on sound research.

3 Know yourself

We have seen the need for a business audit as part of the marketing planning process and, during difficult times, businesses must be even more alert to their own strengths and weaknesses. The key issue is to be *objective*: too many businesses flatter themselves regarding their strengths and underestimate their weaknesses. Being honest with oneself provides a sound basis for dealing with change during tough times. It is documented that managers can be 'myopic', failing to see how changes in demand can affect their products. We must guard against this problem.

4 Make sure your segmentation is right

Customers may be changing in the more difficult environment, and such changes are likely to create new market segments. Parts of one segment may now be more or less attractive to our business (e.g. some customers' disposable income may not be as adversely affected as others' in the segment), and our business has to respond to such changes. Our current marketing research is critical to produce up-to-date information, but we have to be able to act on this information to target redefined market segments. Failure to do this may have a marked effect on business success.

5 Heighten your responsiveness and flexibility

These two qualities are interrelated, and are of particular value to a business during difficult economic conditions. We have pointed to the need for up-to-date information regarding customers and competitors, but without willingness to be responsive and flexible to changes, obtaining such information becomes an arid academic exercise. One of the main threats for any manager during such times is inertia – simply carrying on as before – but if we do this we will be at a competitive disadvantage.

6 Stress the benefits of your offerings

Products and services carry benefits that must match the perceived needs of the customer to facilitate an 'exchange'. During difficult economic conditions customers are more likely to review their buying decisions, including looking at alternative ways of meeting their perceived needs. This presents our business with both a threat (to our current customer base) and an opportunity (where competitors' customers may now be interested in our offerings). Again, we need up-to-date information to ensure that we select the right strategic responses to the current situation.

7 Know your customers' thoughts about price and value

In difficult economic conditions, customers become more price sensitive and seek to maintain the same benefits at a lower cost. They will shop around for the same product at a lower price, or may 'brand switch' to an alternative, cheaper brand from their routine purchases. In 'price-dominant' decisions the customer simply buys the cheapest product regardless of differences in benefits; in 'best-value' decisions the customer weighs up the benefits and cost of each offering and looks for the best value, i.e. the most benefits at the lowest cost. Marketers must know how their customers are thinking about price and value.

8 Get promotion right

Communicating with the market is important at any time, but marketers need to be even more flexible and adaptable when planning their promotional strategies. The marketer has to be ready to change messages and media to respond to customers' needs and competitor actions. Shorter-term campaigns are required to enable the business to redirect resources as required.

9 Take action

The ancient Greek proverb 'Think slowly, act quickly' is particularly relevant during difficult economic conditions. We will have less time available to plan and the consequences of making a wrong decision will be more acute, but failure to act will ultimately put our business at a competitive disadvantage. Marketers have to use information to reduce risk in decision making, but must not be paralysed into inaction through lack of 'perfect' information. We can only reduce risk: there is always an element of risk, but inaction places our destiny in the hands of others.

10 Monitor and control outcomes

All good planning systems link outcomes to the set objectives, and during difficult times this is paramount. For many businesses, the time frame for monitoring outcomes and objectives becomes much shorter: for example, we must assess price changes or promotional messages in a matter of months and then revise our strategies accordingly.

Finally, the marketer must keep an eye on the PEST environment. Many of the factors driving the harsh economic conditions are outside the control of the business but must be understood by the business. We must assess the different PEST conditions prevailing and consider our likely responses to these.

Answers

Sunday: 1c; 2b; 3c & d;
4a; 5b & d; 6c & d; 7d; 8a;
9b & d; 10c.
Monday: 1b & d; 2c & d; 3a;
4d; 5b & d; 6a; 7b; 8d; 9a;
10c & d.
Tuesday: 1c; 2d; 3a & b; 4a;
5d; 6a & c; 7c & d; 8d; 9c;
10b & c.
Wednesday: 1c; 2a; 3d; 4b;
5b; 6a; 7b; 8d; 9d; 10a & b.
Thursday: 1c; 2a & c; 3a & b;
4d; 5d; 6a; 7a; 8b & d; 9c;
10a & c.
Friday: 1c; 2b; 3b; 4d; 5d;
6c; 7a; 8c; 9a & c; 10d.
Saturday: 1a & b; 2a, b & c;
3b & c; 4a, c & d; 5c; 6a,
b & c; 7b, c & d; 8a & d; 9b;
10a & b.

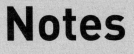

Notes

ALSO AVAILABLE IN THE 'IN A WEEK' SERIES

BODY LANGUAGE FOR MANAGEMENT • BOOKKEEPING AND ACCOUNTING • CUSTOMER CARE • SPEED READING • DEALING WITH DIFFICULT PEOPLE • EMOTIONAL INTELLIGENCE • FINANCE FOR NON-FINANCIAL MANAGERS • INTRODUCING MANAGEMENT • MANAGING YOUR BOSS • MARKET RESEARCH • NEURO-LINGUISTIC PROGRAMMING • OUTSTANDING CREATIVITY • PLANNING YOUR CAREER • SUCCEEDING AT INTERVIEWS • SUCCESSFUL APPRAISALS • SUCCESSFUL ASSERTIVENESS • SUCCESSFUL BUSINESS PLANS • SUCCESSFUL CHANGE MANAGEMENT • SUCCESSFUL COACHING • SUCCESSFUL COPYWRITING • SUCCESSFUL CVS • SUCCESSFUL INTERVIEWING

For information about other titles in the series, please visit
www.inaweek.co.uk

ALSO AVAILABLE IN THE 'IN A WEEK' SERIES

For information about other titles in the series, please visit www.inaweek.co.uk

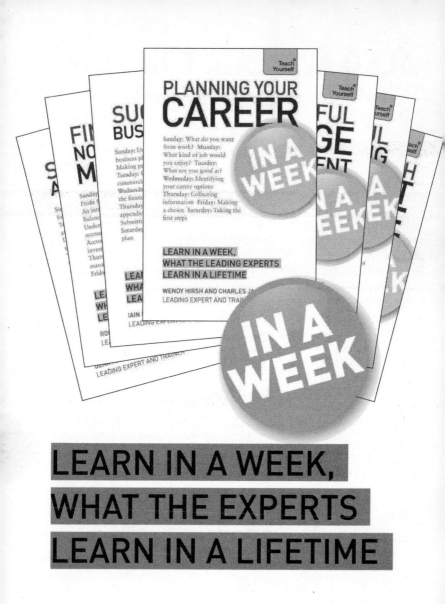

LEARN IN A WEEK, WHAT THE EXPERTS LEARN IN A LIFETIME

For information about other titles
in the series, please visit
www.inaweek.co.uk